CW00739563

BECCLES and BUN

A Portrait in Old Picture Postcards

by

Sylvia and Michael Porter

S. B. Publications

1990

Dedicated to our Godson, Nicholas.

First published in 1990 by S. B. Publications

19 Grove Road, Seaford, East Sussex, BN25 1TP

Reprinted 2000

© Copyright 1990 S & M Porter & S. B. Publications

ISBN 1 870708 51 2

Typeset and printed in Great Britain by Geo. R. Reeve Ltd., Wymondham, Norfolk NR18 0BD.

CONTENTS

CONTENTS CONTINUED

CONTENTS CONTINUED

FOREWORD

Having had the privilege of viewing "A Portrait in Old Picture Postcards" of Beccles and of the villages to the north and south of the town, I would like to say how impressed I am by the quality of the postcards shown and I feel sure that they will generate a great deal of interest for many readers.

They have been collected over many years by Sylvia and Michael Porter, with only one objective – to raise monies for charities.

I am certain that their decision to compile a book, using the postcards, under the heading "A Portrait in Old Picture Postcards", will not only give enthusiasts a lot of pleasure but will raise quite a substantial amount of royalties for Beccles and DitchinghamHospitals.

I wish Sylvia and Michael every success.

Robert E. Ellwood
Mayor of Beccles, (May 1989/May 1990)
April 1990

FOREWORD

It gives me pleasure to write a foreword to this book. Bungay is rich in history and tradition. The office of Town Reeve – the only one in Great Britain – is an embodiment of that aspect of our town. I am honoured to hold the office this year, for the second time.

In the section of the book devoted to Bungay, I would draw the reader's attention to the castle and the Butter Cross. The former is under the care of Bungay Castle Trust and the Friends of Bungay Castle are raising money for the preservation of the ruins. The Butter Cross was rebuilt after its destruction in the fire of 1688 and, this year, we are celebrating the tercentenary of the completion in 1690.

I hope the reader will enjoy this book and be encouraged by it to visit Bungay to enjoy its charm and character.

Mary Kent
Town Reeve of Bungay, 1990

PREFACE

The family of Suckling claims a Saxon origin. In the Saxon language, Suckling – or, as the name was anciently written, Socling – indicated a person holding his estate by socage, or the tenure of the plough.

My aunt, Laura Lucy Suckling was born on 11th September, 1890 in Hungate Lane, Beccles. Later the family moved to Swines Green, Beccles where three brothers and a sister were born. She was an early Edwardian postcard collector. She married Arthur Gorham, a motor-lorry driver but died at the early age of twenty-six years on 1st November, 1916 and buried in Beccles cemetery. This branch of the Suckling family originated from Woodton. My father, Edgar Maurice Suckling, born on 26th June, 1904, inherited her collection and, when I was a small child, he gave it to me.

Michael and I married in 1964 and, up until 28th April, 1977, we had never thought about seriously adding to the postcards and forming our own collection. The item which started it all was an article written by Clement Court (Eastern Daily Press), after which several readers contacted us and encouraged us to join the Norfolk Postcard Club. One person who helped us greatly was the late Mr. Fred Rogers who travelled to the London Postcard Fairs for his own collection and purchased Beccles postcards for us.

Michael and I have sorted out Aunt Laura's collection; of her early greeting cards, only her special ones have been put with ours; her early Beccles cards have been added to our Beccles collection and her Norfolk and Suffolk cards – our speciality – have been placed in our Norfolk and Suffolk collection. All the remaining postcards have been placed in the original album and are still in our possession.

Our postcards have raised money for numerous charities. All the royalties from this book will be donated, on a 50/50 basis, to:-
THE FRIENDS OF BECCLES & DISTRICT WAR MEMORIAL HOSPITAL and
THE ASSOCIATION OF FRIENDS OF ALL HALLOWS HOSPITAL, DITCHINGHAM.

THE LANGUAGE OF STAMPS

It was not until I was sorting out the postcards for this book that I noticed that Aunt Laura had used "The Language of Stamps" on the postcards that were postally used. As we have the above postcard in our collection, we thought it would be a good idea to include it in our book, so that other postcard collectors can have fun lookling at the back of their postcards. The above postcard was published by the Regent Publishing Co. Ltd., and is no. 4714.

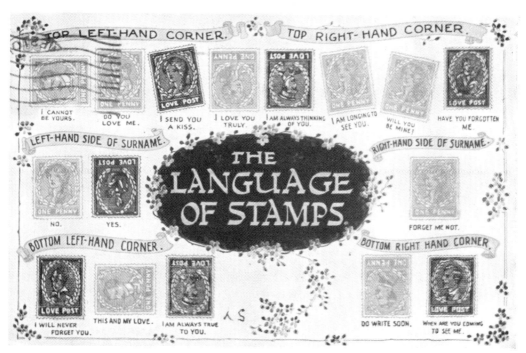

ACKNOWLEDGEMENTS

The authors wish to thank the following people without whom this book would not have been possible:-

Dr. Cane, for the text on pages 56 and 77–82;
Christopher Reeve and Frank Honeywood for the text on pages 57–76;

Mr. Alan Atherton, Chief Librarian, Eastern Counties Newspapers Ltd.;
John Buchanan, Secretary, Barsham and Shipmeadow Parochial Church Council;
Ivan A.W. Bunn, for information on the "Barsham Ghost";
Mr. Frank Denson, Beccles Archivist;
Mrs. Phillippa Simms, Norfolk Heraldry Society;
Mr. Leslie Spall, for details of the Beccles football team;
Suffolk Record Office, Lowestoft;
Lowestoft Library;
Superintendent Registrar, Lowestoft,

Mrs. V. Wisker,
Mrs. Butcher,
Mrs. Wright,
Miss J. Wright,
Mr. J. Gale,
Mr. R. Etteridge,
Mr. and Mrs. Thorby,
Mrs. C. Clarke,
Mrs. G. Mills,
Mr. Rolph,
Mr. L. Jones,

Gillian Jackson, for editing the text;
Steve Benz, for additional editing and marketing.

INTRODUCTION

Beccles is a town with a long history. It is mentioned in the Domesday Book, where it is listed as having a church, a market and a herring fishery. The manor and advowson of Beccles were granted to the Abbey of Bury Saint Edmund's by King Edwy, about the year 960. At this period, it is supposed the tract of marshes extending from Yarmouth to some distance above Beccles was a broad estuary. Some years afterwards, probably by the shifting of the sands off the coast, the mouth of the estuary began to be obstructed, and the sea to be excluded; in consequence of which, the extent of the marshes was gradually increased, and, in the process of time, rendered fit for the pasturage of cattle.

By the middle of the thirteenth century, a bridge had been built over the River Waveney and Beccles had two market places – Old Market and New Market. The town's position beside the river has been an important influence on its history. Being bounded by marshes on three sides, most recent development has taken place on its southern edge and has left much of the oldest part of the town intact. Despite two serious fires in the sixteenth and seventeenth centuries, many historic buildings have survived, and the street plan can be likened to that of a mediæval town – narrow streets, winding lanes and connecting alleyways.

Beccles is dominated by its most-noted archictectual landmark – the detached bell tower of St. Michael's Church. In Ballygate stands Sir John Leman's school, dating from the seventeenth century and one of the finest buildings in town, although it is no longer used as a school. Many Georgian buildings have also been preserved. A large part of the old town has been designated as a conservation area. Where modern development or conversion has been necessary, this has – for the most part – been carried out in a sympathetic manner. In 1979, Suffolk County Council, Waveney District Council and the Department of the Environment jointly inaugurated a scheme to restore and maintain buildings of historical or special architectural value, within the conservation area. The opening of the Beccles bypass has ensured that the town does not have to suffer the constant flow of heavy through traffic, and it has since been possible to introduce pedestrianisation, where appropriate.

INTRODUCTION CONTINUED

This volume shows the town as illustrated on picture postcards. These were introduced in Britain in the 1890s and the majority of these illustrations are from the beginning of the twentieth century – the "Golden Age" of the picture postcard. There were many large firms who published postcards on a national basis and covered places throughout the country. However, their views usually depicted the main streets, historical landmarks, churches and rural scenery. In contrast, local photographers often produced the best views of an area. Not only did they issue postcards showing the main streets, but also produced views of residential areas, industrial scenery, local events and disasters, transport and local people and personalities. Such postcards were not usually issued in great numbers and are, therefore, much sought after by postcard collectors and local historians, today.

The first section of this book covers the town and the surrounding areas of Beccles. The postcards have then been chosen to follow a route westward through the villages of Barsham, Shipmeadow and Mettingham, before a selection of views of Bungay. From here, across the River Waveney, the route returns eastward via Ditchingham, Broome, Ellingham, Kirby Cane, Geldeston and Gillingham.

The compilation of this book has been most enjoyable and informative. We hope that the reader will derive as much pleasure from these pages as we derived from their preparation.

Sylvia and Michael Porter,
Worlingham,
Near Beccles,
May, 1990

THE COAT OF ARMS
OF BECCLES, c. 1905

Beccles was not granted a coat of arms until 1951. However, at the time of the publication of this "Ja-Ja" postcard, the representation illustrated here was often used. It was taken from an old civic seal, on which there was a church and the words "Sigillum concilii municip Becclesiae" (Seal of the Municipal Council of Beccles).

The Domesday Book refers to the town as "Becles" . The origin of the name is the old English "Bœce" (a stream) – hence beck, and lœs (a pasture, meadowland). Other early spellings include: Becclys, Beckell, Beckles, Becles, Beclys, Bekelis, Beklie, Beklis, Beklus and Bicolys. In 1901, the population was 6,898.

THE OLD MARKET, BECCLES, c. 1910

The buildings surrounding the Old Market have not changed a great deal since the beginning of the twentieth century. The Old Market is now used as a bus station which is very convenient for quick access to the town centre, St. Michael's Church, the swimming pool and the River Waveney.

NORTHGATE, BECCLES, c. 1912

This very narrow street leads from the Old Market to the River Waveney. On the left of this view is the Lord Nelson public house, selling Morse's Fine Ales and London Stout. The small building beyond, with a finial on its apex, is a garage. On the right-hand side, the first shop is Line's butcher's shop; further along is Fenn's, a tailor and clothier, and, next door is a bakery. The people are standing at the entrance to Wilson Pathway, which leads to Ravensmeer. At one time, Sir Claude Auchinleck (1884–1981) lived in this street; following distinguished service in the Middle East and Burma, during World War 2, he was promoted to Field Marshal in 1946.

Beccles Bridge, built partly of materials from Ingate Church, about 1437; demolished 1884.

THE OLD BECCLES BRIDGE

As stated on the postcard, this old bridge was demolished in 1884. It was replaced by a new bridge, which carried the main road from Beccles to Norwich, until the new bypass was opened. The buildings in the background have all been demolished.

BECCLES QUAY, c. 1908

Beccles has a beautiful riverside, with plenty of mooring places. Its regattas were very popular in the early part of the twentieth century and brought many visitors to the town. They are still an important annual event in the town and are now preceded by a carnival in early August. The wooden building, on the left of this picture, has now been demolished. On the right is Darby's woodyard; the tall chimney still stands. Today, there is a Broads Information Centre, toilets, souvenir shop, play area for children and a large, grassed quay.

THE GREAT FLOOD AT BECCLES, August, 1912

Beccles was not the only town to suffer from the floods – they also reached several other places, including Norwich and Homersfield. Many postcards depicting the damage were issued. This one is a "multi-view" and shows scenes around the town. *Top row, left to right:* Gillingham Dam, Bridge Street and Fen Lane. *Middle row, left to right:* Avenue Marshes, a general view and Thurlows Yard, with another view of Gillingham Dam on the bottom. The children have taken advantage of the unexpected opportunity for a paddle!

THE CHURCH OF ENGLAND MISSION ROOM, RAVENSMEER, c. 1912

This hall – which could seat a hundred people – was situated on the corner of Denmark Road. In 1979–80, it was converted to a bungalow and is now called Corner Cottage.

STATION ROAD, BECCLES.

14163

STATION ROAD, BECCLES, c. 1912

In the centre of this picture, a horse-drawn Great Eastern Railway delivery cart approaches the cameraman. The railway station is just visible in the distance. On the right-hand side, the spire marks the Wesleyan Chapel, built in 1872, and since demolished; two houses now occupy the site. Behind the tree is the Baptist Martyrs Memorial Chapel, founded in 1808 and re-erected in 1890. The three Beccles martyrs, Thomas Spicer, John Denny and Edmund Poole, were burned at the stake nearby. On the extreme right is Gales Travellers and Commercial Hotel which was converted to a garage in c. 1960. In 1983, this was replaced by a car showroom which opened in 1984.

CORONATION PROCESSION, STATION ROAD, BECCLES, 22nd June, 1911

This procession of youngsters and a few adults is making its way to the Common for the celebration to mark the Coronation of King George V. Station Road is decorated with flags at most houses; the road is seen here looking in the opposite direction to that on the previous picture. In the background is the Assembly Room, a large building that is used for a variety of public functions. It was held in trust by the Mayor, to whom all applications for use were made. The Assembly Rooms are now known as the Public Hall and bookings are made through the Waveney District Council.

9

S 6524   G. E. R. STATION (INTERIOR) BECCLES

THE GREAT EASTERN RAILWAY STATION, BECCLES, c. 1905

When the people of Beccles celebrated the coming of the railway in 1853, a verse was recited in honour of the man responsible: "A better time is looming in the distance borne onward swift on Peto's golden wing. Already we behold with Heaven's assistance, the brightly dawning day he has come to bring. Welcome, welcome, friend of rich and poor." The railway station opened in December 1854. On 8th February, 1855, a special train brought visitors from Halesworth to the English Glee and Madrigal Union at Beccles Assembly Room. The town's new gas-lamps were lit for the first time that night. The bay platform, on the left of this view, served the Waveney Valley line. The waiting-room and first footbridge have now gone, and only the left-hand track remains.

BECCLES AVENUE, c. 1909

In 1863, an avenue from Station Road to the Common was laid out by the Corporation, at a cost of about £1,000. It is sixty feet wide and a quarter of a mile long. Elm trees, shrubs and flowers were planted along each side and the whole is enclosed by iron railings. As a result of the 1912 floods (see page 6), many trees were uprooted and destroyed. More recently, the 1987 hurricane caused further damage to the trees.

BECCLES MALTINGS FIRE, 1912

These maltings were situated in Gosford Road. The photograph was taken after the fire was extinguished. It was a serious fire, causing a great deal of damage. Local residents who can recall the disaster remember that rats ran from all directions! In this picture, the firemen involved in the clearing up work have paused for a moment to pose for the camera; the incident has attracted a small crowd of curious bystanders. On the opposite side of the street is the Star public house. The maltings have now closed.

BECCLES HOSPITAL, FAIR CLOSE, c. 1914

The Hospital was erected in 1874, at a cost of approximately £1,500, on a site presented by John Crisp, Esq. In 1887, two wards were added, at a cost of £400 and, in 1900, there were fifteen beds available. The building still stands, but has been converted to private residential accommodation.

Sheepgate, Beccles.

92599.

EXCHANGE SQUARE AND SHEEPGATE, BECCLES, c. 1908

On the left-hand side of this view is Gunn & Hill's hardware shop, with a superb array of their wares displayed outside. On entering the shop, one was greeted by a small, white-haired gentleman and, whatever item was requested, he would find it! Next door is Lloyds Bank and, beyond, Poultons, a boot and shoe shop. The awning on the opposite side of the road is at White's, a jeweller's shop. The building on the right was the Post Office, whch later became Star Tea Supply. The old Corn Exchange still stands behind Lloyds Bank, the entrance being in Exchange Square; for a while, it was used as a theatre. Sheepgate is now a pedestrianised area.

"BLYBURGATE UNDER SIEGE" BECCLES, c. 1910

Several men are involved in extensive road-works, which, as usual, have attracted a crowd of onlookers! This scarce photographic postcard also clearly shows the premises of E.M. Harper, a furnishing and ironmongery store. On the right is Pearce's Store, selling groceries, wines and spirits. Beyond is the sign denoting the Red Lion public house. Further along, and shown right centre background, was the Labour Exchange, which has since been converted into flats.

Beccles.

Blyburgate.

BLYBURGATE, c. 1905

This view of the street is looking towards the town centre and St. Michael's Church – the opposite direction to the previous page. Behind the wall on the left are the gardens of Crowfoot House. The premises on the right are Watsons, a chemist – many local people can remember this shop. Further up the street was Leggett's fresh fish shop.

S 6507

COUNCIL SCHOOLS BECCLES

THE COUNCIL SCHOOL, PEDDARS LANE, BECCLES, c.1908

The school was built in 1877. New classrooms were added to both the boys and girls schools in 1895; each of these departments could accommodate sixty children. Today, the building is used as an Antiques Centre. The small, square building on the right was a mortuary!

CLASS IV, THE COUNCIL SCHOOL, PEDDARS LANE, BECCLES, c. 1905

This postcard photograph is from the author's family album so, if any reader went to school with Maggie, Fred, Eddie or Bob Suckling, he may be on it!

BULLOCKS LANE, BECCLES, c. 1910

Bullocks Lane is now known as South Road. The Cemetery is on the left. At the top of the road, on the left-hand side, is Brand's Garage and, just around the corner, is Beccles Sports Centre.

BECCLES AND DISTRICT WAR MEMORIAL HOSPITAL.

BY LEYNEEK BECCLE

BECCLES AND DISTRICT WAR MEMORIAL HOSPITAL, c. 1929

The Hospital was built in 1924, next to the site of the old windmill, on land close to St. Mary's Road and presented to the town by Mr. Alex Elliott. The building costs totalled £13,000 which were raised by public subscription. In 1937, there were 23 beds. The Casualty Department was extended in 1980, with a further extension in May, 1988. A Continuing Care Ward, of 24 beds, was opened in May, 1987. Today, the Hospital also has 24 acute medical and surgical beds, a Physiotherapy Department, an Occupational Therapy Department, a speech therapist and consultants hold Out-Patient clinics here.

THE WAR MEMORIAL, Ocotber 1921

The Memorial is on the corner of St. Mary's Road and Priory Road; it was unveiled on 1st October, 1921. It is twenty-four feet high and has the names of those people lost during World War I on its base. In 1988, the names of those people lost during World War II, and that of one person lost in the Korean War, were added on plaques. These were dedicated at the Remembrance Day Service, held at the War Memorial, that year.

BECCLES WAR MEMORIAL UNVEILED. OCT. 1ST 1921.

ST. BENET'S MINSTER, ST. MARY'S ROAD, BECCLES, c. 1910

A convent of Dominican Nuns of the 3rd Order was founded by Miss Bathurst and established in Grange Road, in 1896. This Roman Catholic church is built in the Romanesque style and was started in 1900. The nave and aisles were completed in 1901 and the sacristies in 1908. The total cost of construction was about £20,000. In this view, the Catholic Primary School is on the right and, behind, there are scaffolding poles that were being used for the construction of the tower. Today, there are houses in the foreground.

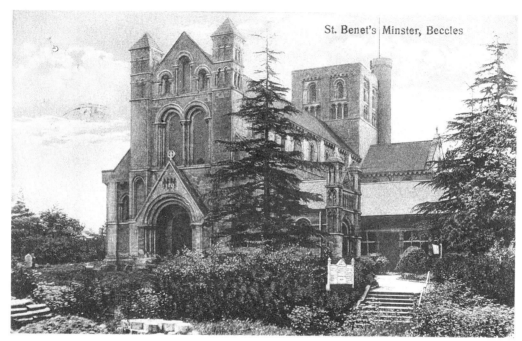

St. Benet's Minster, Beccles

ST. BENET'S MINSTER, ST. MARY'S ROAD, BECCLES, c. 1930
This is a later view of the Minster and shows the tower, which was completed in 1908.

VIEW FROM THE TOWER OF ST. BENET'S MINSTER, BECCLES, c. 1910

The tree-lined road in the foreground is Grange Road. Behind the houses is Priory Road and the tower windmill, which was demolished in 1923. Beccles and District War Memorial Hospital now occupies the site next to the mill (see page 20).

ST. MARY'S CORNER, BECCLES, c. 1905

This postcard shows the beautiful trees that used to grace this approach to Beccles. Unfortunately, as a result of the recent hurricane, many of the trees have been uprooted. This view was photographed from Ballygate, with Ringsfield Road on the left and Bungay Road on the right.

Fauconberge School, Beccles.

7469 The "Wyndham" Series

FAUCONBERGE SCHOOL, BALLYGATE, BECCLES, c. 1904

The building was used as a school from 1846 until 1906. There is an excellent book on the history of this school by E.A. Goodwyn (see bibliography). Today, the canopy has been removed and the building has been converted to council flats. New houses have been built on the right.

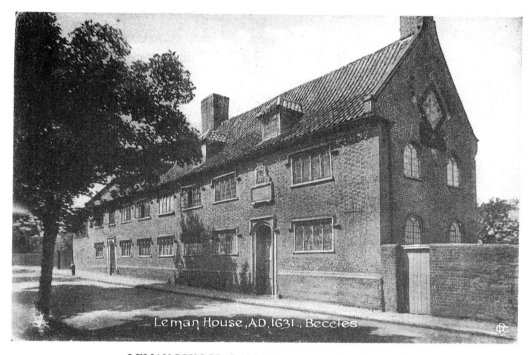

Leman House, AD. 1631., Beccles

LEMAN SCHOOL, BALLYGATE, BECCLES, c. 1910

The Leman School was founded by Sir John Leman, K.T., who, in 1631, bequeathed "a messuage to be used for the School and the Master's House in Ballygate Street and the undermentioned lands etc. to the Corporation of Beccles in trust that the Schoolhouse with the garden and appurtenances should be a Free School for 48 children, 44 of them to be inhabitants of Beccles, two of Ringsfield and two of Gillingham and they should be taught English, Reading, Writing and Arithmetic by a Master and Usher". Today, the house is occupied by two professional musicians who specialise in early Music, and perform all over the world. The School Hall is their music room.

14209   A VIEW OF THE WAVENEY, BECCLES.

A VIEW OF THE WAVENEY, BECCLES, c. 1905

Since the photograph for this postcard was taken, the trees have matured. Looking over the river towards Gillingham and Geldeston, this is a lovely place, especially on a summer's evening when there is often a glorious sunset, which is reflected on the water. Adding to the scene, there may be keen sailors bringing in their boats after a day on the river and local fishermen sorting out the day's catch.

THE CROWN & ANCHOR AND THE ANGEL, BALLYGATE, BECCLES, c. 1910

On the back of this postcard, the following information is given: "The Crown & Anchor and the Angel, Beccles. Standing side by side in ancient Ballygate Street, these two old inns have witnessed much of the passing pageantry of Beccles history. A famous landlord of the former was James Potter, who was also Town Crier, Clerk of the Market and Poulterer".
The old inns are both private houses today.

ST. MICHAEL'S CHURCH TOWER, BECCLES

The Church was built in 1350. The building of this detached bell tower commenced in 1500 and took forty years to complete. It is 97 feet high and has four storeys; it contains a peal of ten bells. In this picture, the Mayor can be seen peering out from the centre of the clock! On the Walk side of the tower, there is a plaque which bears the following information: "Beccles Tower. With this Beccles Penny of 1795 the sixteenth century Tower was bought for Beccles in 1972." Between 1973 and 1977 £68,000 was raised with the aid of public subscription for the restoration of the exterior.

Architects: Feilden & Mawson
Mayor: Ald. E.G. Gilbert, M.C.M.A.
Masons: A.J. Woods & Sons

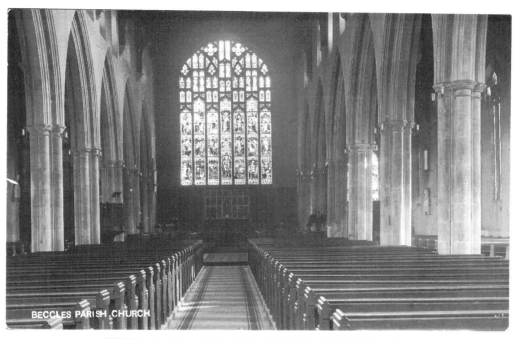

BECCLES PARISH CHURCH

THE NAVE, ST. MICHAEL'S CHURCH, BECCLES, c. 1920

The informative caption on this postcard reads: "The Nave and Chancel are of equal width and height, and their unusual width forms one of the chief features of the church. The original oak screen was destroyed by the fire of 1586 A.D. and the new one was presented to the church in 1919. The large East Window was erected to commemorate the Jubilee of Queen Victoria in 1887 A.D."

Market Place, Beccles

NEW MARKET, BECCLES, c. 1900

This is an early type of picture postcard – the back was reserved for the address and any message was written on the front, usually in a space left for that purpose. In 1902, new Post Office regulations allowed a message to be written on the back, which was then divided to separate message from address. In this view, the shop behind the gas-lamp belonged to Mr. Self, a fruiterer and seedsman. Above it is the office of the East Suffolk Gazette, which was published every Tuesday. A farmer's seed-drill stands outside the next shop, which later became Morlings with a double frontage with a balcony above. On the right, the ironmonger's is Masters & Skevens.

FANCY DRESS PARADE, NEW MARKET, BECCLES, c. 1950

The group of children is lined up for the judging of a fancy dress competition. The winner was Miss Hazel Read, who was dressed as a "Doll in the Box". Behind the crowd on the right is Morlings' music shop, which has since moved back to its original premises in the town. In the background is Durrant's, auctioneers and estate agents.

THE WALK, BECCLES

THE WALK, BECCLES, c. 1950

A more recent postcard of the town is illustrated here because it shows one of the town's well-known shops – Bon Marché. This grocery and haberdashery store was popular with children who loved to watch the money being transported from the counter to the cashier's office, by means of canisters on overhead wires. Beyond Bon Marché are: Keebles, a chemist, and Wilsons' furniture shop. On the left, the café is the Buttery; these premises are now occupied by a branch of the Woolwich Building Society. In the distance is the cinema in Saltgate.

SALTGATE, BECCLES, c. 1920

As can be seen, this used to be a very narrow street. All the buildings on the left-hand side have been demolished. The old cinema stood on the right and, when this picture was taken, a Harold Lloyd film was showing at the time. This building is now John Wilson's furniture shop.

Pudding Moor, Beccles.

PUDDINGMOOR, BECCLES, c. 1929

The name Puddingmoor is said to derive from the mediæval English for frog moor. This is an old part of the town which is still a most enjoyable place for a stroll. On the right, the sign reads "Boats for Hire. H. Mouel". In the distance is the Pickerel Inn, which is now a private house.

THE RIVER WAVENEY, BECCLES, c. 1910

The photographer has captured a delightful picture of this wherry with the white snowcap. Wherries of this size transported cargoes of up to 40 tons. This one is passing the old swimming pool, which was built in 1894 and was 180 feet in length. A new, heated, outdoor pool was built in the 1950s and is a popular attraction in summer. St. Michael's Church tower can be seen in the background.

ROOS HALL, BECCLES, c. 1905

Thomas Colby, who married Ursula Rede, built the present venerable mansion called "Roos Hall". It was probably completed in 1583, as his initials "T.B.C.", along with that date, remain on the waterpipes of the roof. Situated off the Bungay Road, it is constructed of red brick with pedimented windows and step gables. It is furnished with a wide and rather primitive staircase, each step of which is formed from a solid block of oak. Near to the Hall there is a contorted tree that is said to have been used for executions.

The Golf House, Beccles

THE CLUBHOUSE, BECCLES GOLF CLUB, c. 1910

Beccles Golf Club was first formed in circa 1899. It is to the east of the town, on Beccles Common, and has a nine-hole course.

H. Lawrance & Sons, Eastern Counties Mineral water works, Beccles.

H. LAWRANCE & SONS, EASTERN COUNTIES MINERAL WATER WORKS, BECCLES, c. 1908

The works was established in 1860 and was situated in Gaol Lane. The picture shows the office and, on the right, workmen stacking crates. A horse-drawn delivery cart is waiting in the background. The factory site is now used as a car park for William Clowes, the printers.

GREETINGS FROM STEFFANI'S SILVER SONGSTERS.

STEFFANI'S SILVER SONGSTERS, c. 1939

The Songsters appeared at the Regal, which stood in Ballygate but was demolished in 1989. Steffani's real name was Frederick Wisker; his father was a boot and shoe repairer in Beccles. Most of the singers came from Cardiff, with a few from London. In the front row, fourth from the left, is Ronnie Ronalde, who was born in Islington but lived in Beccles for a time. He was well-known for his singing, whistling and yodelling. His best-known songs were "If I were a Blackbird" and "In a Monastery Garden".

41

BECCLES STRIKE, c. 1903

These strikers were obviously happy to pose for the cameraman. It seems that they had probably staged a demonstration – there is a band of musicians in the centre of the group. The placard in the front reads: "Beccles Strike Spreading Romantic Elopement".

BECCLES HARRIERS, 1925–26

The players were – *back row:* C. West, L. Spall, T. Collett, G. Reynolds; *middle row:* G. Took, F. Baldwin, G. Wright, S. Fairweather, F. Squire; *front row:* unknown; C. Green, R. Tricker, F. Austin, Bob Suckling.

THE "LEGGETTONIANS" CONCERT PARTY - BECCLES

THE "LEGGETTONIANS" CONCERT PARTY, BECCLES

The members were – *back row:* Alfred Ling, Pearl Balls, Leslie Balls, Jack Leggett, Edgar Brown and Mr. Bowen. *Seated in the front:* Hilda Mann, Lennie Stevenson on drums and a piano-accordian player whose name is not known.

THE FIRST BECCLES WILD MEN, c. 1935

This photograph was taken at a hospital carnival. Professor Pholto was played by Mr. Samson and the four "wild men" were: Stanley Roe, Herbert Roe, Frank Rivett and Roger Etteridge.

COMIC CARD, c. 1904

The postcard was published by the famous firm of Raphael Tuck & Sons, in their "Oilette" series. It is from a set of six "Motoring" postcards, drawn by Lance Thackeray, the artist. The postcards would have been sold nationally and, where required, could be overprinted with the name of the place in which they were to be sold. A suitable reply to the policeman today might be – "Constable, one cannot exceed the speed limit in this present one-way system!"

THE SHIP INN, 1912

This postcard shows the Ship Inn during the August 1912 floods. The inn was built in the early 1700's and had stabling for 12 horses. The Ship Inn is now the Ship Guest House with Riverside Tea-Rooms. In one of the guest's bedrooms is an original fireplace.

Barsham Church.

7479 The "Wyndham" Series.

THE CHURCH OF THE MOST HOLY TRINITY, BARSHAM, c. 1907

The church tower is built of rough flint rubble, 55 feet high and in two or even three sections. The lower part is of Saxon origin and is 33 feet high; the upper part is Norman and narrower in diameter. The whole of the east wall has an unusual stonework trellis, and incorporates a stained glass window by Kempe. The church has a thatched roof which caught fire in September, 1979. The congregation had to move to Shipmeadow whilst the damaged building was repaired. The thatching and building work was completed in August, 1980, but internal repairs took another three years. Adrian Bell, the author, is buried in the churchyard.

THE INTERIOR, CHURCH OF THE MOST HOLY TRINITY, BARSHAM

In the nave there is a list of the Rectors of Barsham, and the Patrons from 1321 to the present day. Records of earlier rectors have been lost, but it is known that, during the reign of Edward the Confessor (1042–1066), Barsham Church was served by a priest named Leustann. After the 1979 fire, the estimate for repairs to the interior was £45,000. To offset this cost, much of the work was carried out on a "do-it-yourself" basis. The work was completed in March, 1983.

BARSHAM RECTORY, c. 1910

The Rectory stands some distance from the road – close to the church. This view shows the house in 1910, whilst the cover illustration shows it in the 1930s. It was the birthplace of Maurice Suckling and his sister, Catherine, who married the Reverend Edmund Nelson in 1749; their son was Horatio Nelson. The Rectory is now a private residence. Closer inspection of the cover picture reveals the figure of the cook, in uniform, standing on the right. This lady was to be the future Mrs. Edgar Suckling, the author's mother (see Preface). In 1979, she was invited to the Rectory by the owners, Mr. and Mrs. Meo, and told them about her life in their house during the 1930s.

"THE GHOST OF BARSHAM", c. 1905

A very unusual postcard! An ingenious local photographer used his imagination to create this picture from an ordinary photograph, taken on the Bungay road. It is strange that the message on the postcard of Shipmeadow Church refers to the ghost; it reads: "Dear L, are you going to see this ghost any more. I know you are a T.T. but that do not matter . . .". The apparition shown here seems to be female. There is no record of such a ghost but there are reports of a phantom coach and six horses, seen near the site of Barsham Hall, which used to stand nearby. The coach is said to carry "Old Blunderhazard" and travels every Christmas Eve, just before midnight.

SHIPMEADOW CHURCH, c. 1906

This postcard is from Laura's collection (see Preface). The Church is built of brick and flint with a Tudor west tower. Services ceased in 1977, because of lack of use. In 1978, Parish meetings were held to discuss the repairs required and to decide the future of the building. It was agreed that the church be declared redundant. It was officially closed on 1st January, 1981, with future services to be held at the Church of the Most Holy Trinity, Barsham.

Mettingham Church & the "Tally Ho" Inn.

THE CHURCH AND TALLY HO INN, METTINGHAM, c. 1905

All Saints Church is an ancient building. The north doorway is a good example of Norman workmanship, with very rich dog-tooth moulding. The round tower contains four bells. The Tally Ho Inn dates from the beginning of the nineteenth century. It was originally a public house with an adjoining terrace of three cottages.

Mettingham Castle Gateway.

7431 The "Wyndham" Series.

THE CASTLE GATEWAY, METTINGHAM, c. 1905

The castle was built by Sir John de Norwich, who died in 1361. The gatehouse and picturesque, ivy-clad ruins show it to have been a fortress of considerable extent and strength. In 1880, a red-brick mansion was built within the ruins. Six silver bells were found in the moat. In recent years, much of the growth has been cleared from the stonework, in order to avoid further deterioration.

METTINGHAM HALL, c. 1910

The Hall was built in c. 1660. It has fine curved Dutch gables and a moat. This postcard was sent from someone at the Hall and the message on the back reads: "This is the back of the house. I will send you the front later on. Queen Elizabeth has stayed here. Such a glorious old place and beautiful views. You will see the moat, it runs round the house".

THE CASTLE, BUNGAY, c. 1950

The original castle was built by Hugh Bigod in 1165. Just ten years later, he was forced to surrender his fortress by Henry II. In 1294, Roger Bigod rebuilt the castle as an octagonal shell, with round entrance towers – as seen in this picture. It once had a 70-feet-square keep – the height of St. Mary's Church tower, which can be seen in the background. This view of the thirteenth-century gatehouse towers shows the temporary, wartime fence, which was not removed until 1958. The ruins have since been restored.

THE MARKET PLACE, BUNGAY, c. 1910

Market day, believed to have been established by royal decree in 1382, is still held here every Thursday. The Butter Cross was rebuilt after the Great Fire in 1689–90, with the lead statue of Justice being added in 1754. The cage used for the detention of prisoners was removed from beneath the Cross in 1836; the steps on which butter, eggs and poultry were displayed for sale were removed in 1863. To the left of and behind the Butter Cross, the old Crown Hotel can be seen.

S 6136

MARKET PLACE, BUNGAY

THE MARKET PLACE, BUNGAY, c. 1900

The town pump, in the centre, was used by the street-waterers, whose job it was to dampen the dusty roads, in the days before tarmacadam was introduced. The two pump handles swung backwards and forwards – not up and down – and would be operated by two people at once. In 1935, the pump was replaced by the Black Dog standard, on which a plaque records the visit of "Old Shuck, the fearsome Black Dog of Bungay. All down the church in midst of fire, the heilish monster flew; and passing onwards to the quire, he many people slew". (The dog had appeared in the parish church, during a thunderstorm in 1577).

CORONATION CELEBRATIONS, MARKET PLACE, BUNGAY, June 1911

The people are gathered to celebrate the Coronation of King George V. The Market Place has been decorated with bunting. The town band is in the centre of this picture. One group of spectators is assembled on the balcony above Wightman's shop; most of the first-floor windows that overlook the Market Place have people looking out at the proceedings. Chase's butcher's shop can be seen on the left, in Trinity Street, adjacent to the Queen's Head Hotel.

H. WIGHTMAN & SON, MARKET PLACE, BUNGAY, c. 1920

Henry Wightman acquired these premises for his drapery business in 1861. When he died in 1903, the business was continued by his son, Ernest, who eventually went into partnership with his eldest son, Ronald. The family of F. R. Wightman also ran a clothes shop in St. Mary's Street. Once again, the balcony is decorated, but there is no indication of the occasion being celebrated.

THE OLD POST OFFICE, MARKET PLACE, c. 1905

Originally situated on the corner of Chaucer Street, the Post Office moved to this site in 1897 and, in the 1940s, moved again to its present position in Earsham Street. These premises were formerly occupied by William Adkin, a gunsmith. On the right of this picture, in Bridge Street, the sign for the Queen's Head Hotel is visible.

BRIDGE STREET, BUNGAY, c. 1914

When this photograph was taken, the street was a busy pedestrian thoroughfare, supporting a large number of shops; its character has now been altered by the onslaught of heavy motor traffic. In this view, five public houses can be seen. In the right foreground, the Queen's Head Hotel and the Green Dragon; on the left, the Beaconsfield Arms and, further down the street, the Chequer's and the King's Arms.

The Mill Stream, Bungay

THE MILL STREAM, BUNGAY, c. 1909

This was a man-made cut, supplying water to power Marston's Mill. In about 1960, it was filled in when the site was taken over for Greene's boatyard. Bungay is located on a loop of the River Waveney – almost making it an island. The origin of the town's name is probably – "island of Buna's people". In the Domesday Book, it is given as Bungeia and Bunghea.

HOLY TRINITY CHURCH, BUNGAY, c. 1920

The tower is believed to date from the Saxon period, and is the oldest surviving building in the town. The south aisle is fourteenth century, and the chancel was rebuilt in 1926. The gravestone inside the railings commemorates Major General Robert Kelso, who died in 1828. The "table" tomb next to it commemorates the Burtsal family.

Trinity Church, Bunga... ...ith's, Series) J 2603.

THE INTERIOR, HOLY TRINITY CHURCH, BUNGAY, c. 1920

The picture shows the church before the chancel was rebuilt in 1926. The pulpit, recorded as being set up in 1558, is seen here under the arch, between the nave and aisles. At present, it stands between the memorial tablet and window on the left of this photograph. In 1952, this window was altered and enlarged as a thank-offering from the Sunday School.

ST. MARY'S CHURCH, BUNGAY, c. 1920

The Church was once attached to the Benedictine Priory, founded in 1183, by Roger de Glanville and his wife the Countess Gundreda. The Priory was dissolved in 1539, and the ruins can be seen on the left. The tower dates from the fifteenth century and has polygonal buttresses and turrets. The Church suffered considerable damage in the Great Fire of 1688. The railings in the foreground enclose the memorials to John Barber Scott and his family.

INTERNATIONAL STORES, ST. MARY'S STREET, BUNGAY, c. 1920

The original International Stores was on the corner of Priory Lane, in premises recently occupied by Rebecca's restaurant. Many stores had postcards produced, showing the shop front and, as in this case, the staff as well. This photograph, taken by the local firm of Clarke, also shows a wealth of detail in the well-filled window displays. Today, this shop is occupied by Londis, a supermarket.

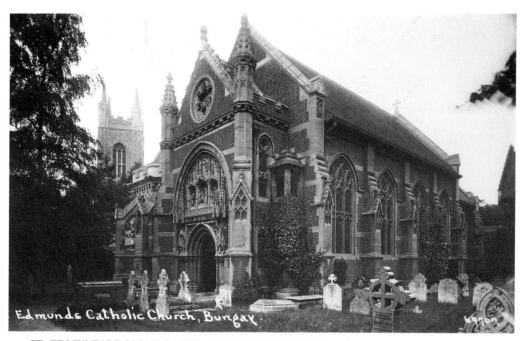

Edmunds Catholic Church, Bungay.

ST. EDMUND'S ROMAN CATHOLIC CHURCH, ST. MARY'S STREET, BUNGAY, c. 1910

The first church was built on land belonging to the Duke of Norfolk, in 1823. It was rebuilt in 1892, with a more elaborate facade, designed by Bernard Smith. The work was financed by Frederic Smith, a local solicitor, who also financed the adjoining Catholic School.

ST. MARY'S STREET, BUNGAY, c. 1904

In the 1860s, this road was known as Olland Street. This view – from the south – shows the comparatively new Catholic School, on the right, with St. Mary's Church tower in the background. On the extreme left is the sign of the Prince of Wales public house. In the distance is H.W. Short's stationery and printing shop, now Martin's, the newsagents.

S 6135　　　　　　　　LOWER OLLAND STREET, BUNGAY.

LOWER OLLAND STREET, BUNGAY, c. 1910

On the right railings front Nursey's, stonemasons, yard. Further along, on the same side, is the Ship public house. St. Mary's Church tower is just visible above the rooftops. A man on a horse-drawn water-wagon is busy damping down the dusty road.

UPPER OLLAND STREET, BUNGAY, c. 1920

The photograph was taken from a position outside the wall of the former Holy Trinity Rectory on the right. On the left, the Rose & Crown public house is seen after it was rebuilt in mock-Tudor style, in 1913. It is now a fish and chip shop. Note the telegraph poles, which had only recently been installed when this photograph was taken.

EARSHAM STREET, BUNGAY, c. 1920

The shop on the left, now the Mint House, was formerly occupied by several Bungay photographers, including the Clarkes – father and son. Further along, on the same side, the striped pole denotes the premises of Trett, the "Demon Barber". At the end of the street, on the right, is the old Grammar School. On the corner of Chaucer Street, the pump is just visible behind the trees.

CHAUCER STREET, BUNGAY, c. 1920

In earlier times, this street was known as Two Brewers Street, named after the public house which once stood on the right, at no. 6. This view was taken looking towards the printing works. The building on the left is the one occupied by the Post Office between 1827 and 1887. The Centenary Rooms, with their elaborate design, were built in about 1911.

WEBSTER LANE, BUNGAY, c. 1912

On the corner of Popson Street, this is now known as Webster Street. In the centre of this picture is the Chaucer Institute, erected in 1909 by Clay's, the printers; it stands on the site of the old Popson almshouses. The tall chimneys, on the left, belong to the old Tudor House. Sadly, this was demolished in the 1950s and the site is now used as a car park.

COCKS & SON, EARSHAM STREET, BUNGAY, c. 1921

This grocers, drapers and costumiers store stood next to the old Grammar School, the site of which is now the Post Office. These windows are packed with a variety of goods, from tinned foods to rolls of carpet. The main building, on the left, is now occupied by the Bungay Bookshop. Note the cobbled surface on the side of the pavement – these still survive on the corner of Chaucer Street.

ST. MARY'S SCHOOL, EARSHAM STREET, BUNGAY, c. 1910

The building was formerly a fine private house called "The Lindens", which dates from the early eighteenth century. It became a girls' school in the mid-nineteenth century, firstly run by Miss Owles and, later, by Miss Maddle. In the 1920s, it became co-educational with a preparatory department for boys. The school closed in 1966 and is now a residential home for the elderly.

BUNGAY AND WAVENEY VALLEY GOLF CLUB, c. 1905

The clubhouse shown on this postcard is a larger version of the original corrugated-iron building of 1889. It continued to cater for Bungay golfers for nearly a century and has now been replaced by a much bigger brick building. Golf is played over a large area of Bungay Common and the Club now has 600 members. This building backed onto the old railway station and a signal can be seen to the right of the clubhouse. The line has now been replaced by a fine straight bypass.

House of Mercy. Ditchingham.

THE HOUSE OF MERCY, ALL HALLOWS, DITCHINGHAM

The House of Mercy was part of the original All Hallows Convent of Anglo-Catholic nuns founded in 1854 by Lavinia Crosse the daughter of a Norwich surgeon. It was a penitentiary, the purpose of which was to "rescue fallen women from the streets". It was later called "St. Michael's House", where the Sisters educated and cared for disturbed children. In recent years this function has also ceased and the building has become a Retreat House for the Community.

ALL HALLOWS HOSPITAL, DITCHINGHAM, c. 1910

This view shows the back of the men's ward and the hospital chapel. It was built in 1873, by the Anglo-Catholic Community of All Hallows. Although not under the National Health Service, it still functions as a small cottage hospital serving Bungay and district. It has been fully modernised and is staffed by highly-qualified nurses and the local family doctors. Major surgery is carried out by visiting consultants from the Norfolk & Norwich, and Gorleston hospitals. Nearby, there was one of the earliest public bath-houses provided by John King in about 1730.

THE CHAPEL, ALL HALLOWS SCHOOL, DITCHINGHAM

The original All Hallows School Chapel was built in the early years of the twentieth century but was converted later to a school library. A new chapel, dormitories, classrooms and a swimming pool have all been built since World War 2.

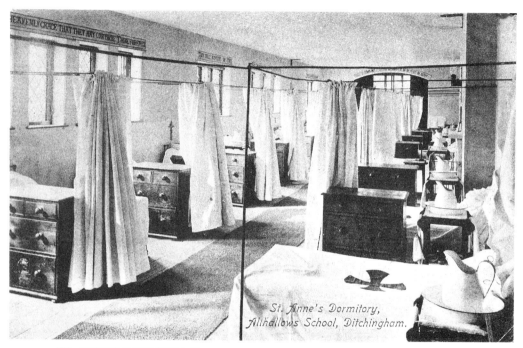

ST. ANNE'S DORMITORY, ALL HALLOWS SCHOOL, DITCHINGHAM, c. 1905

This view of the first All Hallows School dormitory can be dated by the absence of electricity and plumbing! Despite this, each cubicle appears to be well-equipped with the basic necessities. Note the religious texts above each window.

THE REFECTORY, ALL HALLOWS SCHOOL, DITCHINGHAM, c. 1905

From the evidence on this postcard the dining room of the school seems to have been able to seat about twenty pupils. Numbers had reached sixty by the outbreak of World War 2 and later rose to two hundred. The original orphanage of the Community was founded in 1865 but became a boarding school for girls fifty years later. The Junior School also took day girls and a few boys from time to time. During World War 2 they were taught at nearby Hedenham Hall.

BROOME SCHOOL, c. 1910

The school was built in 1875, at a cost of £900. It could accommodate ninety children. It is now closed as a school, and the building is used as a tea room and antiques shop.

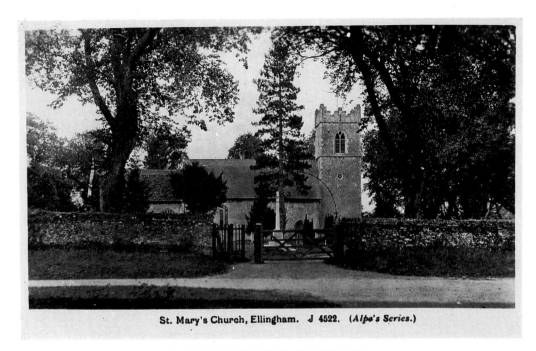

St. Mary's Church, Ellingham. J 4522. (*Alpe's Series.*)

ST. MARY'S CHURCH, ELLINGHAM

The church is situated on the north bank of the River Waveney, 2 miles east north east of Bungay. It has five bells, which are chimed, but these are static whilst the clapper strikes the sides of the bells. The church has some very fine stained glass windows.

ALL SAINTS CHURCH, KIRBY CANE, c. 1907

All Saints Church is an ancient structure of flint, in mixed styles, and consists of a chancel, nave, north aisle, south porch and a round, embattled, western tower containing five bells. The tower was repaired in 1925, at a cost of approximately £130. The south doorway is a good example of the Norman style.

THE MEMORIAL CHAPEL, KIRBY CANE, c. 1907

The three young boys are posing whilst the photographer takes his picture of the David Pilgrim Memorial Chapel and its extension, where a commemorative stone reads: "Wesley Chapel 1849". Later, another extension was built behind the wall, where the trees are in this picture. Several stones were laid with various names and the year – 1922 – carved upon them. A memorial hall, used as "a Club and for Amusements and Entertainment", was erected in 1921. It was presented to the community by J.R. Crisp, Esq.

Hart's Hill, Geldeston.

HART'S HILL, GELDESTON, c. 1911

For this postcard, the village was photographed from the Beccles to Bungay road, on the Norfolk side of the Waveney valley. There is now an estate of council houses and bungalows in the fields on the right.

"Our Lady of Perpetual Succour",   Gillingham. (Norfolk.)

THE ROMAN CATHOLIC CHURCH, GILLINGHAM

The Roman Catholic Church was erected by the late John G. Kenyon, in 1838, and completed in 1902. It is an edifice of red brick, with stone dressings, in the Italian style, and has one hundred and twenty sittings.

ST. MARY'S CHURCH, GILLINGHAM, c. 1912

St. Mary's Church is a building of flint, in the Norman style. It consists of an apsidal chancel, nave, aisles and a tower containing three bells. The Church was enlarged in 1858 and there are now one hundred and eight five sittings.

GILLINGHAM STREET, c. 1913

These houses had only recently been built when this photograph was taken. The house on the right is Number 44. The next two pairs of semi-detached dwellings are Providence Villa and Princess Villa, and both bear date stones for 1911. The last house in the row is Number 64. Some children are playing in the street outside this house. This part of the village has changed very little.

BIBLIOGRAPHY

Suckling's History and Antiquities of the County of Suffolk, Volume 1.

White's Norfolk, 1890.

White's Suffolk Directory, 5th Edition.

Kelly's Directory of Suffolk, 1900.

Kelly's Directory of Norfolk, 1912.

Kelly's Directory of Norfolk/Suffolk, 1937.

Suffolk Churches and their Treasures, 1st Edition, by H. Munro Cautley.

North-East Suffolk, by Alan Jobson.

East Suffolk Illustrated.

East Suffolk Railway, by J.M. Cooper.

The Fauconberge School, Beccles, 1770–1926, by E.A. Goodwyn.

St. Michael's Church, Beccles, 3rd Edition, a leaflet by George S. Odam.

All Hallows, Ditchingham, by Sister Violet.

Bungay Castle Guide, by Dr. Hugh Cane.

The Church of the Most Holy Trinity, Barsham, 1977.

White's Suffolk, 1855.

Local titles published by S.B. Publication in the series – "A Portrait in Old Picture Postcards".

Peterborough, Vols. 1, 2 & 3
The Villages of Old Cambridgeshire
Wicken – a fen village.
Huntingdonshire, Vols. 1 & 2

Hertfordshire, Vols. 1, 2 & 3

From Highgate to Hornsey
The Parish of St. Mary, Islington

Watercolours of Norfolk Past

Norwich Vols. 1, 2 & 3
The Norfolk Broads
Holt and District
Thetford, Brandon and District
West Norfolk
Great Yarmouth, Vol. 1

Beccles and Bungay
East Suffolk

General titles: The Blue Funnel Line
Liverpool to North Wales pleasure-steamers
The Magic of Multiples: Twins & Triplets on old picture postcards
Constabulary Duties: A history of policing.

For full details about other titles available and in preparation write (enclosing a S.A.E.) to:-
S.B. Publications, 5 Queen Margaret's Road, Loggerheads, Nr. Market Drayton, Shropshire, TF9 4EP.